THE BA
BORN IN A STABLE

LUKE 2:1-18 FOR CHILDREN

Written by Janice Kramer

Illustrated by Dorse Lampher

ARCH Books

LIBRARY OF CONGRESS CATALOG CARD NO. 65-15145
MANUFACTURED IN THE UNITED STATES OF AMERICA

ISBN 0-570-06013-3

Not quite two thousand years ago
the emperor decreed
that all the world must be enrolled....
LET NO ONE FAIL TO HEED.

(The world was quite mixed up, you see,
and no one seemed to know:
how many people WERE there? And
what taxes did they owe?)

Throughout the earth the rich,
the poor, the young, the very old,
all traveled to their towns of birth
so they could be enrolled.

And so it was, to Bethlehem
a man named Joseph went
to list his name and see how much
he owed the government.
Beside him Mary traveled, too.
Not once did she protest
how long and hard the trip had been,
how much she needed rest.

In Bethlehem they found the inn
and knocked upon the door.
"My rooms are filled!" the owner yelled,
"I haven't any more!"
When Joseph told him quietly
of gentle Mary's plight:
that she would have a baby soon,
perhaps that very night,

the owner stood in thought and rubbed
his bushy bearded jaw.
"I'll let you have the stable, then.
You'll have to sleep on straw."

So Joseph and his wife unpacked
and settled down to rest
not caring that they couldn't have
the biggest and the best.
They ate their supper slowly as
they watched the sun go down,
and yawned as darkness fell at last
upon the little town.

The night was silent. Everyone,
it seemed, was fast asleep
except for shepherds in the fields
who had to watch their sheep.
They huddled close and whispered low
to keep themselves awake.

Then suddenly their eyes grew wide —
their knees began to shake.
For there, above them in the sky,
an angel did appear.
The glory of the Lord shone down,
and they were filled with fear.

No longer did the shepherds quake
with anxious fear and dread,
and when the angels disappeared
the shepherds quickly said:
"Oh, let us go to Bethlehem
and find the manger bed!"
And off across the fields they ran —
to Bethlehem they sped!

The manger wasn't hard to find,
and there the shepherds' eyes
fell on a sight that filled their hearts
with wonder and surprise:

For there was Joseph, standing tall
and gazing down with care
upon his blessed Mary and
the baby lying there.

"A wondrous child!" the shepherds cried
in voices of delight.
"See there — around him shines a strange
and heav'nly looking light.
How warm and bright it seems against
the coldness of this night!
He surely is the one we seek;
the angel's words were right!"

To Mary and to Joseph and
to everyone they saw
the shepherds told the story that
had filled them with such awe:
"This baby is the Promised Prince,
the Mighty Lord,
the King.

We know because tonight we heard
the holy angels sing.
They told us that this blessed child
of low and humble birth
was truly Christ, the Son of God,
the Savior of the earth!"

The news was spread from town to town.

The whole world must be told
till every person,

rich

or young

or poor

or very old,

has heard about the coming of
the Savior of all men,
whom God has sent to earth because
of His great love for them.

A CHILD'S CHRISTMAS PRAYER

Be near me, Lord Jesus;
I ask Thee to stay
close by me forever,
and love me, I pray.

Bless all the dear children
in Thy tender care,
and take us to heaven
to live with Thee there.

Dear Parents:

Have you ever had the feeling that your child is confused at Christmastime? There is such a mixture of reindeer, Santa Claus, presents, parties, angels, and unreal mangers. What are we really celebrating, and why? How did it all happen?

Our book is intended to help parents and children remember the real story of the first Christmas and the love of God behind it. Our heavenly Father sent us a Savior who did not shrink from being poor and unrecognized. Christ wasn't even born in a house. We often forget this and tend to be too romantic about the manger in the stable. Mary and Joseph had a hard time of it! The shepherds who welcomed the Christ Child were the nobodies of society in that day. Our God chooses hard and strange ways to win back His children. This is why Jesus came. He saves us from the power of sin and brings God's life back to us.

This is the Good News, and really the only reason we celebrate Christmas. Without it we would have only empty trimmings. Will you help your child see the heart of Christmas by making the first Christmas come alive for him and by centering the season in the birth of Christ?

THE EDITOR